HOW IT GOES

MOTORCYCLES

Kate Scarborough

BARRON'S

First edition for the United States,
Canada, and the Philippines published
1994 by Barron's Educational
Series, Inc.

Designed and produced by Aladdin
Books Ltd
28 Percy Street
London W1P 9FF

First published in
Great Britain in 1993 by
Watts Books
96 Leonard Street
London EC2A 4RH

All inquiries should be addressed to:
Barron's Educational Series, Inc.
250 Wireless Boulevard
Hauppauge, New York 11788

ISBN: 0 8120 1994 6

Scarborough, Kate.
How it goes, motorcycles / Kate
Scarborough.
p. cm. – (How it goes)
Originally published: How it goes,
motorbikes. London: Watts Books, 1993.
Includes index.
ISBN 0-8120-1994-6
1. Motorcycles–Design and
construction–Juvenile literature.
[Motorcycles.] I. Title. II. Series.
TL440.15.S33 1994
629.227 5–dc20
CIP AC 94-1801

Design: David West
          Children's Book
          Design
Designer: Keith Newell
Editor: Olive Prettejohn
Researcher: Emma Krikler
Illustrators: Ian Thompson
              Simon Tegg

Printed in Belgium

CONTENTS

Here is a table to help you
understand the measurements
used in this book.

1 kilometer = 0.62 miles
1 meter = 3.28 feet
1 centimeter = 0.39 inches
1 liter = 0.26 gallons
1 ton = 1.02 tonnes

INTRODUCTION

The first motorcycles were ordinary bicycles with very basic engines fitted onto them. They have since developed into a very popular form of transport and have many different uses. Modern motorcycles, compared to earlier ones, have more powerful engines, better brakes, and tougher tires, and they travel faster. They are also safer to ride. This book explains how motorcycles work and shows their different uses.

MR. FIXIT
To help you learn about riding motorcycles, watch out for Mr. Fixit. He will point out all the important things you should know.

WHY MOTORCYCLES?

In the Western world, the motorcycle has become a sophisticated means of transportation. It is ideal in busy cities with congested traffic. In developing countries, the motorcycle is often the only affordable form of transportation. For the enthusiast, there are many types of competitions to participate in.

A POLICE BIKE
With so much traffic on the roads today, it is difficult for police to reach an emergency quickly. Motorcycles are an excellent solution.

WORLD WAR I MESSENGERS
During World War I, motorcycles were used regularly to carry messages. During World War II German motorcycles even had sidecars with machine guns on them.

MESSENGER BIKES

In cities there are hundreds of businesses. Although they can communicate by mail and fax, motorcycle messengers are often used for sending official documents as they are fast and reliable.

PARAMEDICS

In an emergency, it is important for a medical person to be on the scene as soon as possible. Motorcycles can weave their way through traffic, so they are able to get to accidents quickly.

TWO-WHEELED BALANCE

Can you remember when you learned how to ride a bicycle? Or maybe you haven't tried it yet? It is not that easy. You have to learn how to balance when traveling at high speeds on two wheels, especially when turning a corner or going over bumpy ground.

SPINNING WHEEL

If you roll a coin across the floor it will stay upright until it runs out of energy. The same is true of a spinning wheel. As long as the engine supplies energy, the wheels are more likely to stay upright.

CORNERING

When you turn a corner at high speeds you might think you should lean away from the corner, so that you don't fall into the bend. However, to keep their balance, riders always lean into the corner as shown below.

STUNT RIDERS

Very experienced riders, like the one above, have excellent control and are so good at balancing that they can perform stunts such as jumping off ramps, as illustrated here.

WATCH OUT!

It is all too easy to lose control on a motorcycle, especially if you are traveling fast around a corner. Even if you are very experienced, you can fall and hurt yourself. You have to learn how far you can lean into a bend before the bike's balance is upset.

THE WORKING PARTS

Motorcycles are made up of hundreds of different parts, some large and others very small. Each part is vitally important in making the machine work. You can divide them into systems – fuel, brakes, transmission, suspension, and ignition. These systems work together to make the motorcycle go.

HANDLEBARS
The rider of the motorcycle holds onto the handlebars and uses them to steer the vehicle.

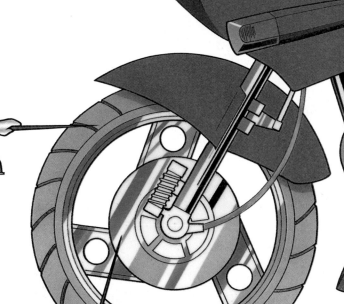

FAIRING
This is a molding that curves around the front of a bike and the rider's legs. It streamlines the bike to help it move faster.

TIRES
Tires are the motorcycle's contact with the ground. The surface of a tire is called its *tread*.

DISC BRAKES
These are fixed to the wheel. When applied, pads press against the disc. This stops the wheel from turning.

CLUTCH
This connects and disconnects the engine to the gearbox. It can work automatically or manually.

STREAMLINING

When you run, air pushes against you. If you wanted to move faster through the air you would have to change shape and become streamlined. Streamlining means creating an object with no sharp edges, so that air can travel smoothly past it, like this motorcycle.

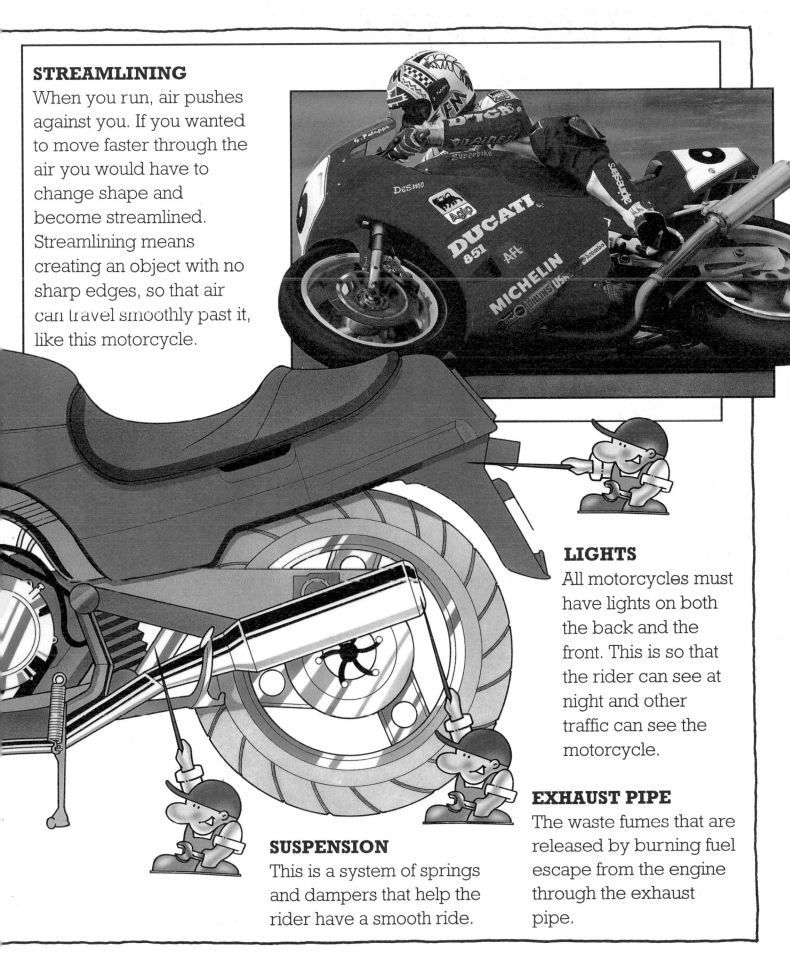

LIGHTS

All motorcycles must have lights on both the back and the front. This is so that the rider can see at night and other traffic can see the motorcycle.

EXHAUST PIPE

The waste fumes that are released by burning fuel escape from the engine through the exhaust pipe.

SUSPENSION

This is a system of springs and dampers that help the rider have a smooth ride.

TWO-STROKE ENGINES

Motorcycle engines normally work with pistons. These are metal tubes that move up and down inside a hollow cylinder. This movement turns the crankshaft. In smaller and simpler motorcycle engines the piston makes two strokes - one up, one down. We call this kind of engine a two-stroke engine.

FUEL
In a two-stroke engine, the fuel mixture contains a lubricating oil to help the engine parts move easily.

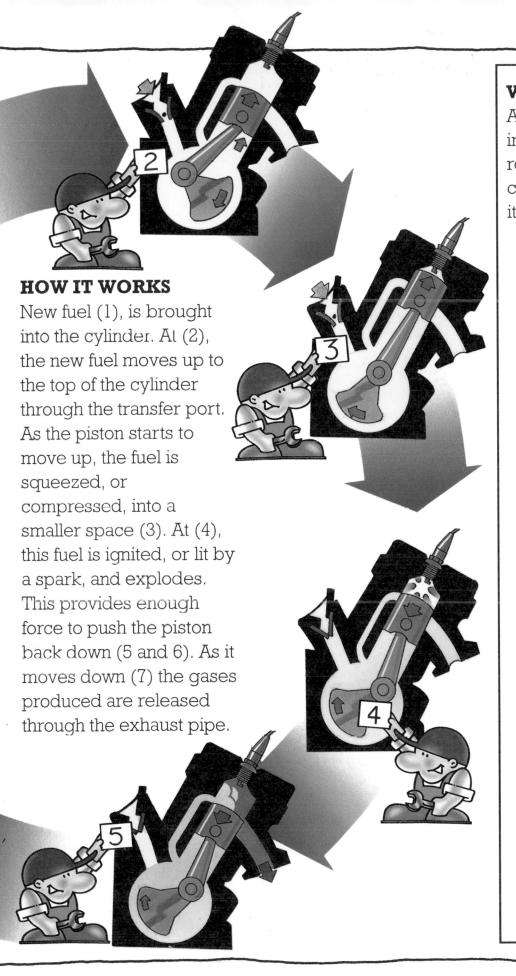

HOW IT WORKS

New fuel (1), is brought into the cylinder. At (2), the new fuel moves up to the top of the cylinder through the transfer port. As the piston starts to move up, the fuel is squeezed, or compressed, into a smaller space (3). At (4), this fuel is ignited, or lit by a spark, and explodes. This provides enough force to push the piston back down (5 and 6). As it moves down (7) the gases produced are released through the exhaust pipe.

WANKEL ENGINE

As the triangular rotor inside the engine rotates, it draws in fuel, compresses it, ignites it, and releases fumes.

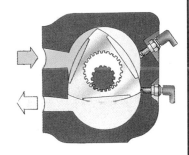

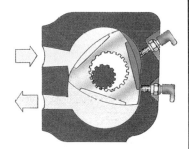

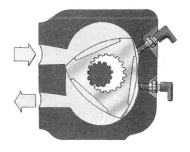

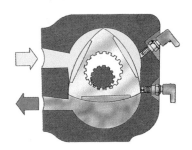

FOUR-STROKE ENGINES

Some motorcycle engines run on a piston engine that uses four strokes to produce power. In general, these engines are more complicated, have more working parts, and tend to be larger in size than two-stroke engines. They also produce less pollution.

FOUR-STROKE ENGINE
The four-stroke engine has valves that let fuel and gases in and out. A chain drives overhead camshafts that control the opening and closing of the valves. There is a lubricating oil around the crankshaft to help the engine parts move easily.

HOW IT WORKS

At the beginning (1), the piston starts its downstroke and the inlet valve opens. The piston continues to move down (2) and draws in fuel through the inlet valve. At (3), the piston starts to move up and the intake valve closes. No more fuel is let in. The piston continues to move up (4), squeezing or compressing the fuel. The spark plug produces a spark that lights or ignites the fuel (5). The gases released force down the piston (6). A new upstroke starts and the exhaust valve opens (7). As the upstroke continues the burning gases are forced out (8). The process is similar to the two-stroke engine, but it uses four strokes up and down instead of two.

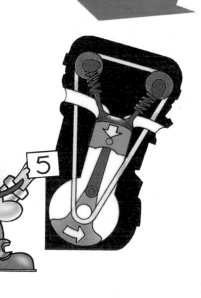

INSTRUMENT PANEL

The largest dial, the speedometer, shows the motorcycle's speed. The RPM (revolutions per minute) counter shows how quickly the engine turns over. The temperature and fuel dials show how hot the engine is and how much fuel is left.

GEARSHIFT

The foot controls this pedal. When the clutch is activated by the left hand, the gearshift is pushed by the foot to change gear. Changing gear can alter the speed of the bike.

THE FUEL SYSTEM

Gasoline flows from the fuel tank into the carburetor. This is a small pot-like unit in which the fuel is mixed with air before it is sucked into the engine and ignited. More powerful motorcycles now use a system of fuel injection.

REAR BRAKE

The right foot operates a brake on the rear wheel. This slows the motorcycle down.

CLUTCH LEVER
When the rider wants to change gear, this lever is pulled back. The new gear is selected and this lever is then released.

INSTRUMENTS
This is where the rider controls the motorcycle. There is the ignition switch to start the engine, all the dials for speed, pressure, temperature, oil, fuel, as well as switches for lights and indicators.

FRONT BRAKE
By pulling this lever back, the rider operates a brake on the front wheel. Most motorcycles have disc brakes on the front wheels.

THROTTLE
When this is twisted back, more fuel is released into the engine.

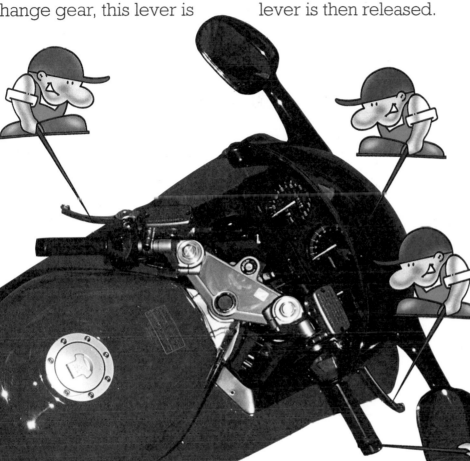

GASOLINE TANK
All engines run on fuel. The fuel is stored on the motorcycle in the gas tank. This is usually found in front of the rider's seat.

RIDING A MOTORCYCLE
As well as balancing on a motorcycle, the rider must control its speed, change gears, and monitor the machine's instruments. To ride the motorcycle, both hands and both feet are used. The instruments on the panel display useful information. The mirrors help the rider be aware of other traffic on the road.

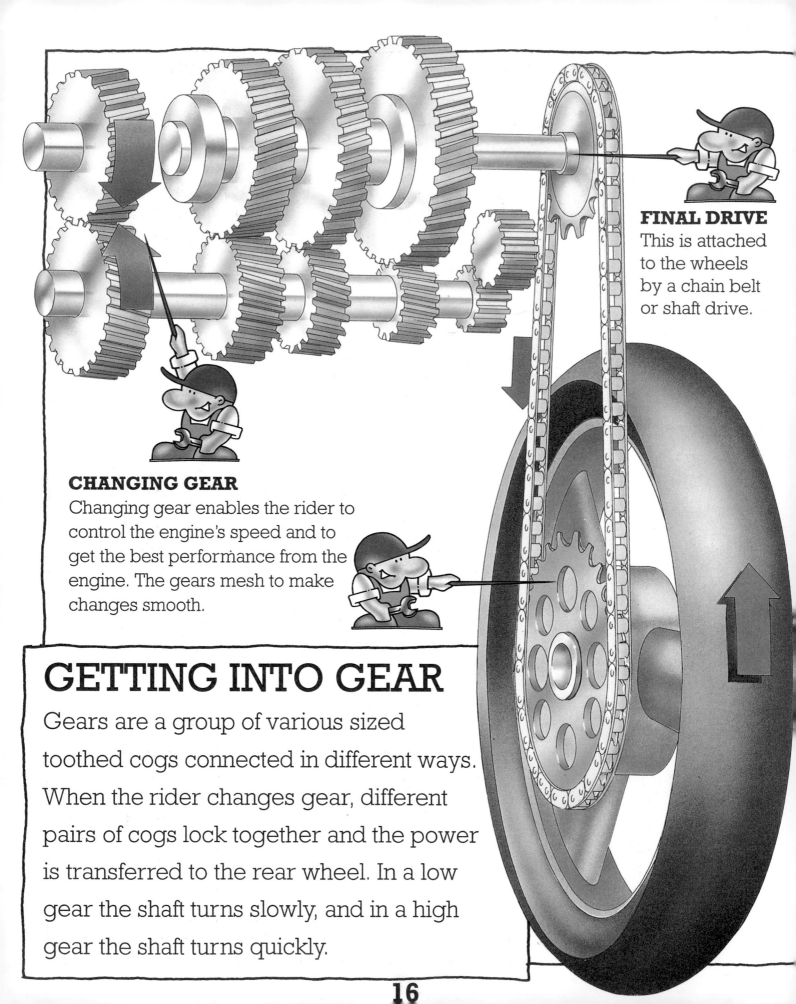

FINAL DRIVE
This is attached to the wheels by a chain belt or shaft drive.

CHANGING GEAR
Changing gear enables the rider to control the engine's speed and to get the best performance from the engine. The gears mesh to make changes smooth.

GETTING INTO GEAR

Gears are a group of various sized toothed cogs connected in different ways. When the rider changes gear, different pairs of cogs lock together and the power is transferred to the rear wheel. In a low gear the shaft turns slowly, and in a high gear the shaft turns quickly.

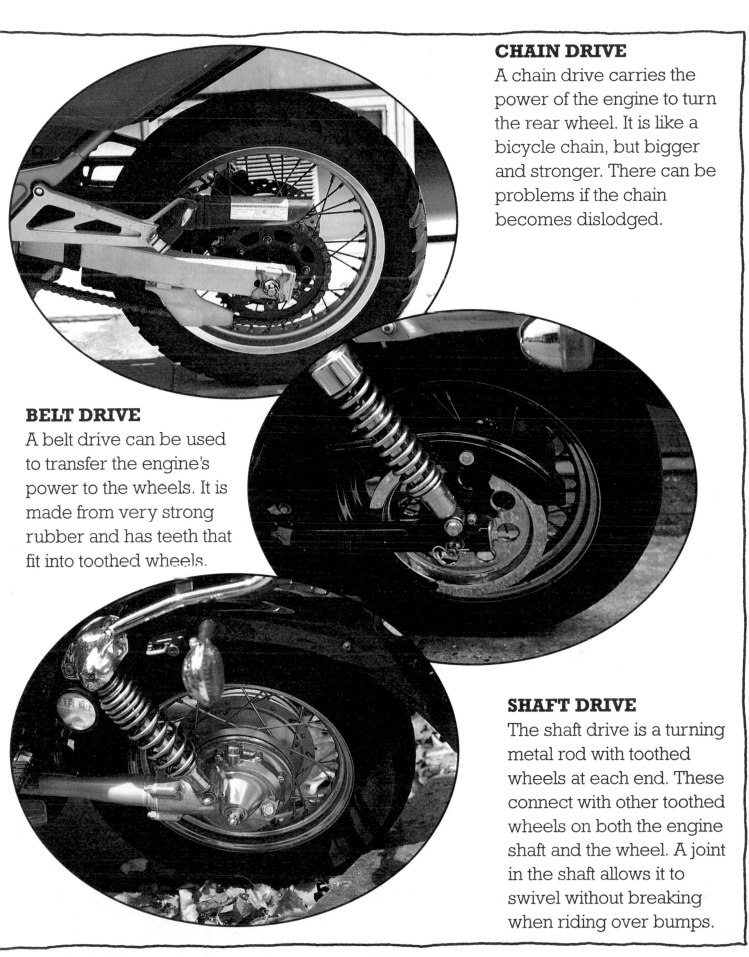

CHAIN DRIVE

A chain drive carries the power of the engine to turn the rear wheel. It is like a bicycle chain, but bigger and stronger. There can be problems if the chain becomes dislodged.

BELT DRIVE

A belt drive can be used to transfer the engine's power to the wheels. It is made from very strong rubber and has teeth that fit into toothed wheels.

SHAFT DRIVE

The shaft drive is a turning metal rod with toothed wheels at each end. These connect with other toothed wheels on both the engine shaft and the wheel. A joint in the shaft allows it to swivel without breaking when riding over bumps.

GRIPPING THE ROAD

The rider has to know that the tires are safe, especially when turning a corner at speed. A tire that has the greater surface area on the ground gives the best grip. Some tires are better suited to particular road surfaces.

FRICTION AND GRIP

Friction is a force that tends to slow down rolling objects. Motorcycle tires must grip the road, otherwise every time the rider rounds a corner, the vehicle could slide out of control. At the same time, tires must not slow the bike down too much. Which surface do you think would make a better tire? The rubber that grips the board as it is raised or the coin that slides down? The rubber has the better grip. There is more friction between the rubber and the board.

TREADED TIRES

In wet weather these are the tires to use. They have channels cut into the rubber or tread. This tread helps to keep the tires on the ground. The water is drained away by the channels in the tread.

SLICK TIRES

These have a smooth tread and hold the road well because more tire touches the ground. They are only used for racing and are not used in wet weather because there are no channels to drain the water away, so they tend to slide.

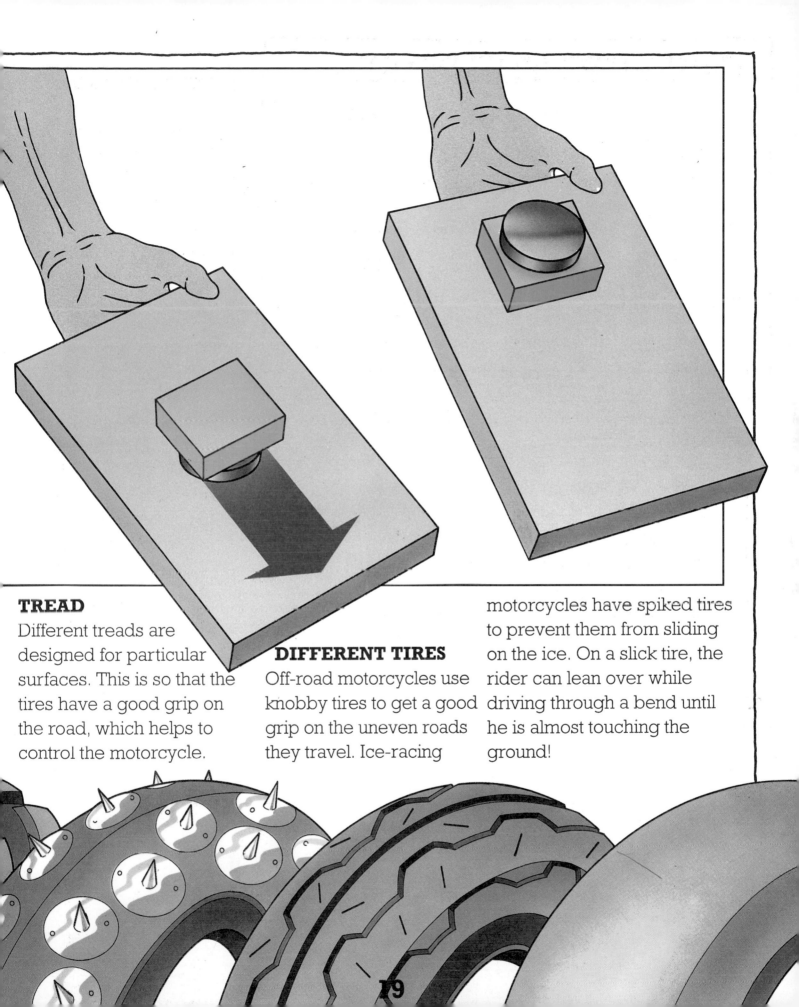

TREAD

Different treads are designed for particular surfaces. This is so that the tires have a good grip on the road, which helps to control the motorcycle.

DIFFERENT TIRES

Off-road motorcycles use knobby tires to get a good grip on the uneven roads they travel. Ice-racing motorcycles have spiked tires to prevent them from sliding on the ice. On a slick tire, the rider can lean over while driving through a bend until he is almost touching the ground!

BRAKING

Motorcycles must have a good braking system because they can travel very fast. Most motorcycles have two separate brake systems. A disc brake on the front wheel, which the rider applies by hand, and a drum brake on the back wheel, which the rider applies using his feet.

MOTORCYCLES WITHOUT BRAKES

Speedway motorcycles shown at right, can be very dangerous. They usually have only one gear and no brakes at all! This means that the rider has very little control over the vehicle especially when turning a corner. As a result, many accidents occur on these motorcycles.

DRUM BRAKE

A typical bowl-shaped drum is fixed to the wheel hub. When the brake handle is squeezed, the brake shoes are pushed against the drum. This forces the wheel to slow down. When the brake handle is released, the springs pull the shoe backs to their normal position.

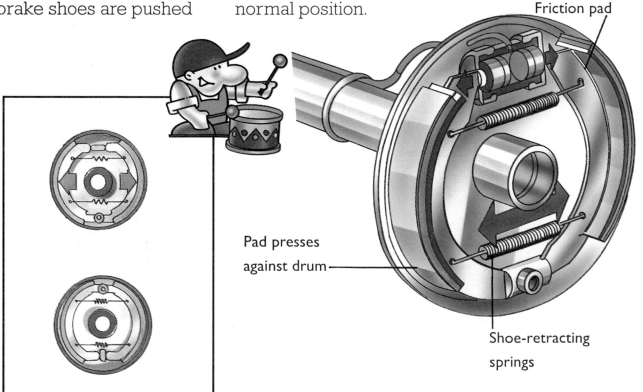

Friction pad

Pad presses against drum

Shoe-retracting springs

DISC BRAKE

Disc brakes work by forcing brake fluid into tubes that produce pressure on the brake pistons.

These then push brake pads against a disc inside the wheel and slow it down.

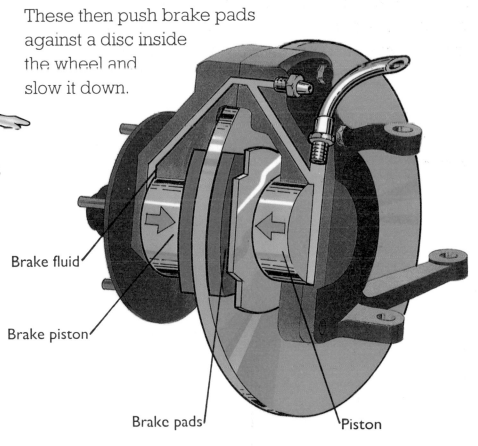

Brake fluid

Brake piston

Brake pads

Piston

TYPES OF MOTORCYCLE

Motorcycles today are all designed for different uses. They are categorized by engine size, measured in cubic centimeters or cc. Racing motorcycles tend to have more powerful engines than motorcycles used for traveling on streets. Touring motorcycles have large engines for coping with long distances.

SCOOTER
Scooters are compact and designed for use at lower speeds.

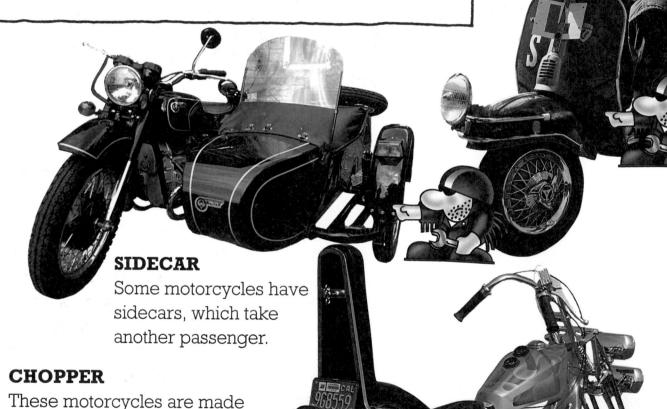

SIDECAR
Some motorcycles have sidecars, which take another passenger.

CHOPPER
These motorcycles are made by their owners who "chop" the original design, and add those features they consider more attractive.

HARLEY-DAVIDSON

This is one of the most famous names in the motorcycle world. Many choppers are based on them. The Harley-Davidson is powerful with a four-stroke engine.

ATV

Cross-country racers can also use the three-wheelers called ATVs. ATV stands for All Terrain Vehicle. With their wide wheels they balance better and can travel faster over rocky ground. They are used a great deal by farmers as well.

SPRING INTO ACTION

It is very important for a rider to have a smooth ride so that the motorcycle is easy to control. Suspension systems allow the wheels to stay in contact with the ground surface as much as possible, and to maintain speed and acceleration.

SUSPENSION

The suspension system helps motorcycles stay level when the wheels ride over bumps in the ground. A motorcycle has two suspension systems, one at the front and one at the back. Both systems work by using springs that act like a cushion. The back suspension is made up of a shock absorber and a spring. It is fitted to the motorcycle's frame and wheel.

FRONT WHEEL SUSPENSION

This is in the wheels' forks. It has springs that move up and down as the tires go over bumps.

MAKE A SPRING

You will need a piece of strong wire and a plastic tumbler. (1) Wrap the wire around the tumbler, making each wrap a little higher than the last one. (2) Pull the tumbler from the wire and cut off the edges with pliers. (3) Press down on your spring. It should bounce back into shape once you lift your hand off.

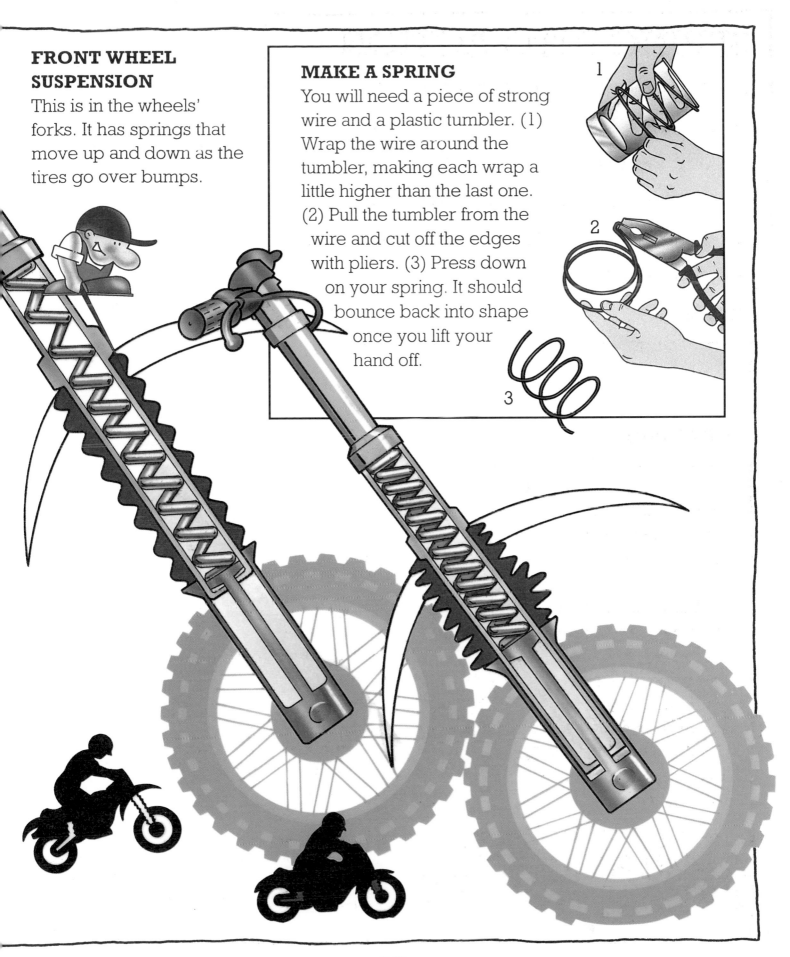

RACING MOTORCYCLES

Motorcycles race in classes according to their engine size. To make them faster they usually have a fairing in the front (see p.8). Some motorcycles have fuel injection or a turbo-charger for more power. There are different kinds of races for the different motorcycles.

(see p.8)

RACING MOTORCYCLES

Racing motorcycles are designed, as shown below, to be streamlined so that they can go faster. They also use slick tires wherever possible.

CROSS-COUNTRY MOTORCYCLES

For cross-country racing, also known as motocross, (see opposite page), tough, lightweight motorcycles are used. They have a raised body, knobby tires, and a very good suspension. These vehicles are made to be especially good at riding over rough terrain.

SIDECAR RACING

This combination is used for speed racing over road surfaces.

MOTOCROSS

Motocross (or scrambling as it is sometimes called) is exciting to watch. The rider uses his skills to race, twist, jump, and turn the bike around a bumpy course.

DRAGSTERS

These are the fastest motorcycles today. They race in straight lines. The position of the rider helps to streamline the vehicle.

FACTS AND FIGURES

THE FIRST MOTORCYCLE

Two French brothers, Ernest and Pierre Michaux, were the first to put an engine to a bicycle in 1868. They used a steam engine to power their bicycle, but this was not a great success.

THE FASTEST MOTORCYCLE

The world record for speed on a motorcycle is 319 miles per hour. It was set by Donald A. Vesco in 1978 in a specially designed streamlined body powered by two Kawasaki engines.

THE MOST EXPENSIVE MOTORCYCLE

One of the most expensive motorcycles ever produced is the Harley Davidson Electra Ultra-Glide. It costs nearly $20,250.

THE LONGEST "WHEELIE"

Yasuyuki Kudoh performed the longest "wheelie" in Tauchiura, Japan, in 1991. He traveled 205.7 miles.

THE MOST PEOPLE ON ONE BIKE

Forty-six members of the Illawarra Mini Bike Training Club in New South Wales, Australia, managed to ride for one mile on a 1000cc motorcycle on October 11, 1987.

THE LONGEST RACING CIRCUIT

The longest motorcycle racing circuit is the Isle of Man TT Mountain circuit. It is over 37 miles long. Carl Fogarty holds the speed record of 123.6 miles per hour for the circuit, set in 1992.

THE FASTEST WHEELIE

The highest speed reached on a wheelie is over 149.8 miles per hour, by Steve Burns at Bruntingthorpe, England in 1989.

THE FASTEST ROAD RACE

In 1977, British rider Barry Sheene averaged a speed of over 135 miles per hour for the 141 kilometer (87.6 mile) 500cc Belgian Grand Prix.

THE MOST IMPORTANT NAMES

After World War II, British motorcycles such as Triumphs and Nortons led the world. But then they were bettered by Italian models such as the Moto Guzzi and MV Agustas. Today the most important names are the Japanese bikes such as Honda, Suzuki, Yamaha, and Kawasaki. These motorcycles prove to be safer, more efficient, and cheaper than their rivals. Other big names today are the "superbikes" such as BMW, Ducati, and Harley Davidson.

GLOSSARY

BRAKES: a system of pads and discs that, on contact with a moving wheel, slow it down. There are drum brakes and disc brakes.

CAMSHAFT: opens valves in four-stroke engines to let fuel in and gases out.

CLUTCH: a lever on the motorcycle that can disconnect the engine from the gearbox during a gear change.

CRANKSHAFT: changes the movement of the piston into a turning movement.

CYLINDER: a hollow tube inside which the piston moves up and down.

DOWNSTROKE: the downwards movement of the piston inside a cylinder.

EXHAUST: the gases that are released by the fuel when it is burned, for which the engine has no further use.

EXHAUST PIPE: the tube where waste fumes from the burned fuel are emitted from the engine.

FRICTION: the force that is produced when two objects rub against each other. It slows down any movement and stops sliding.

FUEL SYSTEM: the part of the motorcycle that holds fuel and sends it down to the engine where it is burned, with air, and releases energy.

GEARS: a group of toothed wheels, or cogs, that can be linked together in different ways. These cogs control the speed of the moving wheels in relation to the speed of the turning engine.

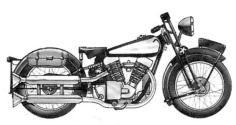

IGNITION: the starting of the engine is produced by igniting the fuel mixture in the cylinders.

PISTON: a metal rod that moves up and down inside a cylinder. It produces power when it is forced down by the burning fuel.

RPM COUNTER: RPM stands for revolutions per minute. The counter shows the revolutions of the crankshaft in the engine.

SHAFT: a bar or rod that turns, or rotates, to transmit power

through the motorcycle. The shaft drive carries power from the engine to the rear wheel.

SPARK PLUG: provides an electric spark that ignites the fuel in the engine's cylinders.

SPEEDOMETER: this dial shows the rider how fast the motorcycle is traveling.

STREAMLINING: is a special shaping of the body of a vehicle so that it moves faster through the air. It offers the minimum resistance to

air traveling past it.

SUSPENSION: is a system of springs and shock absorbers that help to smooth the ride.

THROTTLE: controls the amount of fuel that goes into the engine and so controls the engine speed.

TRANSMISSION SYSTEM: carries power to the front and rear wheels. It includes the gears and clutch.

UPSTROKE: the movement of the piston upwards inside the cylinder.

INDEX